STRATEGIES
FOR SUCCESS
IN THE BAND
AND ORCHESTRA

STRATEGIES FOR SUCCESS IN THE BAND AND ORCHESTRA

MENC MENC
MENC MENC

The National Association for

MUSIC
EDUCATION

This book is based on the principles of instrumental music teaching and the desire to provide a quality experience for our students in school bands and orchestras. We wish to dedicate this book to the teachers who will make this possible—especially to Stephanie Kupchinsky, whose example stimulated the need for a document of this type.

The quotes that appear in the margins of this book are taken from MENC publications and from experts in the field. Full references are in the "Selected Resources" section.

MENC wishes to thank Dorothy Straub, Jacquelyn Dillon-Krass, and Bob Foster for their commitment to band and orchestra directors, especially evidenced in their hard work on this project.

Copyright © 1994 Music Educators National Conference
1806 Robert Fulton Drive, Reston, VA 22091-4348
All rights reserved. Printed in the United States of America.
ISBN 1-56545-038-8

CONTENTS

Introduction

No student's education is complete without music—so no school curriculum can be said to be complete without a comprehensive music program. Such a program offers students experiences that are simply not available through their studies in the other academic subjects. A comprehensive music program includes four balanced, equally strong components: general music classes, chorus, band, and orchestra.

Teachers, administrators, and parents throughout the nation want to offer students access to the incomparable experience of immersion in music making offered by high-quality bands and orchestras. Both the orchestral and band components of a school music program often face challenges in scheduling, gaining administrative support within the overall curriculum, and obtaining appropriate funding. Both bands and orchestras should meet the educational needs of the students and provide exposure to the rich heritage of orchestral and band music.

The challenges of a quality instrumental program, focused primarily on the good of the students, can be met with proper teaching, communication, and administration. This book provides strategies for dealing with issues facing directors of band and orchestra programs. In addition, the quotations in the margins of this book give an idea of the contents of other resources useful in the work of providing instrumental music to students.

This book is based on the combined years of experience of directors who are acknowledged leaders in music education. The information in these pages has been tested in rehearsals; in ongoing relationships with decision-makers, parents, and students; and in contact with thousands of other music educators through the most important professional organizations in the field. Music education professionals should use this information to support and strengthen existing programs and to work for the establishment of programs where they do not yet exist.

This book is a compilation of strategies for teachers to use on behalf of their students—strategies for success.

Teaching for Success

High quality in the teaching of a band and orchestra program is critical to its survival. Where quality instruction is lacking, enrollment usually declines and the administration may consider cutting the program. The challenge, therefore, is to develop a quality program at every level so that the students in the school, the ensemble members and their parents, the school administration, and the community all recognize that the program is successful.

Successful programs share several common ingredients. First, in excellent programs there will be an opportunity for students to study either a stringed instrument or a band instrument. Both orchestra and band programs are essential to a high-quality, comprehensive music program.

Second, it is crucial that both the bands and orchestras at all levels sound good—from the earliest beginners to the most advanced players—so that the students are proud of their membership in the music organization. The repertoire performed in these programs should include music of varied styles and periods and be well within the technical ability of the students.

Where high-quality, substantive instruction exists at every level, fewer students will drop out of the program.

Further, classes at all levels need to be taught by competent personnel who are either specialists in the type of ensemble they direct (band or orchestra) or who have participated in specific study to become specialized in the area they are teaching. It is also equally important that there be an effective, sequential instruction plan in place at every level.

In healthy programs, we find a cooperative working relationship between band and orchestra teachers; in fact, all music teachers in the school system work cooperatively. We also find good parental and community support for the program.

Most important, a successful program is a source of pride to the school and community. This pride starts with the efforts of good teachers—those who continue to learn to perfect and improve their teaching skills throughout their careers. If this happens, students will feel successful and will take pride in being involved in the program.

In the string orchestra, successful programs share some important characteristics. First, it is very important that there be understanding of the unique aspects of stringed-instrument playing (for example, each hand requires a separate technique, and training of the ear is critical). Fewer than 20 percent of school districts in the United States have school orchestra programs in spite of the fact that orchestras are considered major musical and cultural institutions in our society. An orchestral program in a school system is a viable component of a well-balanced music curriculum. With a well-conceived and thorough presentation, administrative decision makers can be convinced that a comprehensive school music program must include orchestra classes.

In the band, successful programs are staffed with strong musicians who realize that band is first and foremost a musical organization that exists to teach children how to express themselves through the creation and interpretation of sound on an instrument. Band teachers must monitor their beginners' selection of an instrument to make sure a child has no physical limitations that could impede his or her success. Physical attributes such as mouth, lip, and teeth formation; overall height; length of arms; and size of hands can all play a part in making sure a child is suited to a particular instrument. Music teachers should also conduct some sort of musical survey or evaluation of each child and share the results with the parents prior to instrument selection. It is also suggested that band teachers consider establishing instrumentation goals to provide for proper balance in the ensembles these children will perform with in later years.

As a child begins to learn a band instrument, the teachers should be patient and thorough in establishing correct hand position and posture habits. Extra time spent on these details as the student begins will pay big rewards as the young musician matures.

● ● ● ● ● ● ● ● ● ● ● ● ● ●
Providing a Rationale

Instrumental programs have been an essential part of the American school music curriculum for generations, yet many school music programs have no orchestras. No school music program can be considered complete without an orchestra. Administrators, educators, parents, and the community at large need to be aware that:

• Every student is entitled to the opportunity to explore classroom music activities, vocal activities, and the study of a band or orchestra instrument during his or her school career.

• Both stringed and band instruments are easily taught. A beginning string group can sound good and can play tunes that both students and parents enjoy after a few lessons—just like the band.

• The literature played by the orchestra and orchestral repertoire transcribed for band represent some of the world's greatest cultural treasures. Classical music is heard and enjoyed on radio, television, and in films, as well as in concert halls around the globe. Performance of great literature is valuable not only for the participants; it also raises the level of cultural awareness in both the school and community.

• Students are attracted to certain instruments because they prefer the sound of string, wind, brass, or percussion instruments. Every child should be given the option of learning to play whatever instrument he or she prefers. (Without a string program, this is not possible.)

- Lifelong opportunities for playing instruments as an adult abound. Community orchestras and community bands welcome capable musicians (especially string players) at the high school level and above. According to the American Symphony Orchestra League, adults in this country have access to some 1,650 orchestras as well as countless smaller ensembles; and there are community bands in almost every population center in the United States.

● ● ● ● ● ● ● ● ● ● ● ● ● ● ● ● ●

Setting Goals

The long-range goals of a band or orchestra program should include:

- Providing for continuous, sequential instruction at each grade level—
  a. technical development on individual instruments
  b. band and orchestral literature
  c. solo and small ensemble experiences.
- Implementing band and orchestra classes in every elementary, middle, junior high, and high school.
- Developing the band and orchestra as integral parts and equal components of the music program.
- Incorporating, by the middle or junior high level, a full orchestra with balanced string sections, woodwinds, brass, and percussion.
- Incorporating, by the middle or junior high level, bands that have complete instrumentation, including piccolos, oboes, bass clarinets, bassoons, French horns, tubas, and a full complement of percussion instruments.

"**M**any people and organizations will help interested educators establish an orchestra program. Do not be afraid to seek assistance. Some suggestions: Call your state music or fine arts consultant.... Visit a successful school orchestra program.... Contact the president of your state music education association.... Contact string-education instructors at state universities.... Don't forget to draw on other school and community resources."

—TIPS: Establishing a String and Orchestra Program

RECRUITING FOR SUCCESS

Students are the heart of the program, and a successful program depends heavily on well-planned, effective recruitment procedures. Recruiting serves to acquaint students with the instruments that will be taught, to guide students in choosing the appropriate instrument, and to inform students about the band and orchestra programs. During recruitment, students should be given printed information about how to enroll, as well as information on specifications of instruments they will need to secure.

In trying to recruit new students, demonstrations (planned with the cooperation of general music teachers and the approval of the school administration) are effective. Present twenty- to thirty-minute demonstrations in individual classrooms, rather than a large demonstration in a school assembly.

Watch for the following elements in all your recruitment demonstrations. Remember that students are a strong influence on other students.

- Present your best student musicians.
- Include a brief demonstration of each instrument that will be taught. After each instrument is heard alone (to demonstrate the characteristic sound), have a group play to show the enjoyment of participation.
- Use your demonstration to balance the instrumentation of the band or orchestra— for example, place special emphasis on the larger stringed instruments (viola, cello, and bass) or on the less popular band instru-

"The personality and enthusiasm of the teacher are the most important factors in influencing a student to play an instrument. Do present the personality that is uniquely yours; don't try to duplicate another teacher's style.

Children respond positively to a teacher who is sincere and reflects a genuine love of children. Positive teacher attitude is vital to successful results in recruiting. Assume the attitude that every child wants to play; your role is to assist them in choosing an instrument."

—TIPS: ESTABLISHING A STRING AND ORCHESTRA PROGRAM

*"*G*ood-quality beginner [stringed] instruments, called student-line instruments, should be shop-adjusted in the United States and follow the MENC minimum standard specifications. These can be found in detail in the MENC publication,* The Complete String Guide.

Once the child is ready for a full-size instrument, parents should be strongly encouraged to upgrade to a "top-line" instrument. Student-line instruments, designed to be sturdy and to withstand the heavy wear and tear imposed by beginning students, cannot produce the kind of tone needed for the more mature music played in middle, junior, or high school orchestras."

—Voices of Industry

ments. Do not be afraid to influence students to choose instruments that will balance the instrumentation.

• Ask students who already play an instrument to encourage their friends to join the program.

Your efforts to recruit students should also involve direct contact with parents. You can provide further demonstrations and discussion about specifics of being in the band or orchestra program at an evening meeting with parents. For this, you will need to reserve space in your school, plan the setup, speak to your school custodian, and arrange for assistance from other music teachers and older students. If the school district permits, invite local instrument dealers to participate in the meeting (they may also offer to help with the daytime recruiting demonstrations to students) and provide printed materials about their rental programs. If you do not have good student musicians from your school to assist you, you could invite students from outside your district, youth symphony members, college students, or private teachers to help you.

Another important element of your recruiting campaign is a letter or brochure for parents describing the pertinent details for starting in the program. This should be distributed to all students in the eligible grades. A sample recruiting letter for orchestra is on page 9; it could be adapted for band. (You may wish to communicate further by telephone with parents of students who do not enroll, but who have been recommended by music or classroom teachers, especially if your recruitment results in fewer students than you anticipated.)

Dear Fifth-Grade Students and Parents:

The Department of Music is offering beginning classes in violin, viola, cello, and bass to all interested fifth-grade students. The classes meet Monday, Wednesday, and Friday for thirty minutes during school hours. Orchestra students can participate fully in academics, athletics, and other activities.

We encourage all fifth graders to sign up for classes. Learning to play an instrument helps students develop creativity and self-discipline, and belonging to the school orchestra opens up a new world of friendship and fun. Instrumentalists can continue to study and perform in middle and high school. After high school, there are abundant opportunities for playing a stringed instrument: university orchestras offer generous scholarships to string players, and many areas have community orchestras. Some students may even choose to pursue music as a profession.

There is no fee for these classes. However, students must provide their own instrument, folding music stand, music book, and a few other inexpensive supplies. Most parents choose to rent an instrument for the first few months of instruction.

Fifth graders interested in learning to play a stringed instrument should come to the school auditorium with their parent(s) on Wednesday, September 3, or Thursday, September 4, between 7:00 and 9:00 PM. Members of the music faculty will be available to answer questions about the program and counsel parents and students on appropriate instrument selection and size; they will also explain how to rent an instrument and obtain supplies. Please fill out the form below and bring it to the session.

Sincerely,

Jane Smith
Supervisor of Music

• •

Date _____

Please enroll my child in the school orchestra program. He/she is interested in playing

_____ or _____ (choose two of these four instruments: violin, viola, cello, bass).

Child's name_____

Address_____

School_____

Phone_____

_____ Previous musical experience_____

Fifth-grade teacher_____

Parent's signature_____

"**B**eginning band instruments are available from a number of reputable manufacturers; however, it is a good idea to have area wind and percussion specialists evaluate all models available and recommend several brands of each type of instrument for your beginners to select.

Directors should also make sure that any student who begins on a "used" instrument does so only after it has been checked over by a reliable instrument technician. Frequently, bad keys, pads, springs, corks, or valves will impair children's ability to create an acceptable tone. Sometimes this can lead to the child dropping out of the program because he or she does not feel musically capable.

As a child develops, the band teacher should not be hesitant to talk to parents about obtaining a "performance quality" or "professional" instrument. Again, directors are encouraged to have an inclusive list of quality brands, makes, and models to give to parents. These instruments will allow the maturing player to continue his or her development of technique and tone quality."

—BOB FOSTER

The recruiting letter should:
• State the value of the program for the child.
• Explain your school district's commitment to the program. Parents need to understand that there is no charge for instruction because the program is part of the school's curriculum.
• Outline opportunities for musicians as adults, including church music, participation in community bands and orchestras, and performance of all types of music, from classical to popular.
• Point out that participation in a band or orchestra will give students an edge when they apply for college admissions. Also mention that there are many scholarships available for instrumentalists—especially for players of string instruments and less common wind instruments.
• Describe the program—what instruments will be taught, when groups will meet, and when classes are to begin.
• Outline performance goals for the year.
• Explain how to enroll, and include an enrollment form.
• Explain how to obtain an instrument and recommend that students rent or lease at first.
• Give the date, time, place, and purpose of the evening parents' meeting and explain how to get additional information.
• Emphasize the importance of parental involvement from the start.

Communicating for Success

Every teacher needs to be aware that ongoing communication with specific individuals and groups is imperative for the success of the program. You will need to continually communicate with administrators, other teachers, the support staff of your school, retail music dealers, students, parents, the community at large, and your professional colleagues.

• • • • • • • • • • • • •

Communicating with Administrators

Get to know your school system's organizational plan immediately, so that you understand the role and responsibilities of each administrator, and your relationship to each one of them. Scheduling, curriculum, testing, facilities, and setting the school calendar require cooperation and communication among staff and administration. If you want your program to be considered a regular part of the school, you must be a regular part of the planning. It is also vital that you be well organized in your job and willing to participate actively in the school community.

You also will need to learn about the chain of command and how the administrative decision-making process works. This will differ from school to school, district to district, and state to state. Critical decision makers in most school systems include:

- the board of education
- the superintendent and assistant superintendent
- the business manager or comptroller
- the personnel director
- the curriculum director
- the music supervisor or coordinator
- the principal and assistant principal
- the dean or guidance counselor

Of course, the administrator of most importance in the instrumental teacher's day-to-day life is the building principal. It is very important for you to keep your principal informed about what you are doing. No administrator wants to be surprised by something happening in the music program without his or her knowledge. Talk to your principal about such things as:

- Approval of the lesson schedule
- The need to change your teaching schedule for a concert in another school
- Plans to attend a professional music educator conference
- Any possible unanticipated expenses
- The theft or loss of any equipment or supplies
- Performances beyond the school day
- The possibility of bringing in a guest artist
- Arrangements for a piano accompanist (if needed)
- Problems with a particular student or class
- Problems with parents
- Problems with people or businesses in the community

In addition, keep an accurate calendar of music events and other school and community events to avoid conflicts. Give your principal a copy of all press releases; letters to parents, teachers, and staff; special activity handouts; and concert announcements before they are distributed. In fact, on important activities, you need prior approval by the principal. This is not only a courtesy but an administrative necessity. It serves to draw the principal's attention to the liveliness and importance of your program, and expresses your interest in being a part of the school. When you work with groups of parents, involve your principal in the development of an appropriate role for booster groups and other organizations for curriculum support, fund-raising, purchases, and social activities.

Work with your principal for a mutual understanding of the proper role of performing groups. Discuss the ways in which your program is an integral part of the total instructional program. Don't forget that the principal will hold you (and all teachers) accountable for the program. Find ways to demonstrate your devotion to student accomplishment, quality, and community service—not just entertainment.

Communicating with Other Teachers

As a member of the teaching staff of a school, it is important for you to get to know all your colleagues, understand their work, and define your role within the framework of the total education of the students. To do this, you should attend faculty meetings and mix with other teachers on a casual basis. For example, make it a point to eat lunch with them occasionally. Do not be guilty of isolating yourself in the music room.

You will find that you have at least one very important interest in common with every teacher in the school—the students. At the elementary level, it is crucial to work with the classroom teachers to identify potential students and to guide those students to the selection of appropriate instruments. As the year progresses, be sure to share the students' musical progress with your colleagues from time to time and thank them for their support, as, after all, they may be allowing students to miss their classes to participate in instrumental music.

Your relationships with other music teachers should be even closer. Work together to develop a school music or arts program calendar. If you share a room, call it a rehearsal or music room—not a band, chorus, or orchestra room. Cooperate with other instrumental teachers, always emphasizing the best interests of the students. For exam-ple, you might recruit together or share wind players between the orchestra and band in the middle school, junior high, and high school. This makes possible full-orchestra experiences for the string players and solo orchestral experiences for the most talented wood-wind, brass, and percussion players. Competing with other music colleagues for students defeats the success of the entire program.

Other music teachers can be of special help in recruiting students for your instrumental program. Talk with your school's vocal and general music teachers to seek their continued support. Ask them to identify talented students who should be included in the program, as well as provide information about individual students and their potential. Also, talk with the regular classroom teachers, asking them to identify leaders and students who are academically capable of adding instrumental music to their schedules. Ask them to remind students to return the application to enroll in the beginning classes.

As a director of an orchestra or band, there are other categories of teachers and educational organizations with whom you must work. These include community music schools, youth and symphony orchestras, and private music teachers. These people and groups encompass some fine instrumental performers. Get them on your team by inviting them to demonstrate, coach, or play a solo with your group occasionally.

Communicating with School Support Staff

It is important to develop a good relationship with school custodians. These people are most willing to help you with such things as opening doors, setting up equipment, readying special facilities, and much more—but this won't happen unless you develop friendships with these people. An expression of appreciation after a special event can pay big dividends later.

School secretaries are other essential people who can help your program run more smoothly. They are the main communication link to the administration and will provide assistance with concert program preparation, telephone calls, schedule changes, special events, and so on. But remember, everyone is asking them for help, so continually thank them for their assistance.

Don't forget to make a special effort to build a good relationship with any teacher with whom you share a room. Keep him or her informed about schedule changes, and agree on responsibilities for setting up and removing equipment, securing the room, and leaving the room clean and orderly. Be sure to express your appreciation from time to time to all the people you work with.

Communicating with Retail Music Dealers

It is most important for you to establish a good relationship right away with the retail music dealers who will be handling instruments for your students. You will need to:

• Learn how your retail dealers' businesses work.
• Communicate to the dealers what you will need, and then recommend all dealers who can supply those needs to students and parents.
• Be sure to include more than one music dealer, if available, in your written communications.
• Become familiar with different brands of instruments. Consider recommending more than one brand. Music dealers will help you to learn about the specifics of different brands.
• Be sure your recruiting letter to prospective students states the instrument specifications that you desire.
• Inform dealers of the recruitment dates for your program and the date on which classes start. Provide dealers with copies of printed materials about enrollment in the instrumental music program. Ask dealers if they have pertinent promotional materials to give to prospective students and parents. Be sure to request these materials well in advance of the recruitment period.
• Be sure to give the dealers plenty of lead time to get products that you want the students to have (two to

three months, if possible). This will help them to have what you want them to have at the correct time.

- Provide detailed specifications for any instruments to be purchased by the school. Don't leave anything to chance. For example, specify brand names and model numbers.
- Establish a repair service with your school music dealers—discuss school pick-up of instruments and loaner availability.

Once you have established a working relationship with retail dealers, communicate with them whenever there are problems. These people have an investment in your program, just as you have an investment in their businesses. As a teacher, you need to always be businesslike and professional in your dealings with retail music dealers.

In the string orchestra, give your dealer a list with your specifications for such things as strings, bows (synthetic hair or horsehair), shoulder pads, endpin stops, length of endpins, etc.

In the band, give your dealer a list of recommended reeds, mouthpieces, ligatures, mutes, valve and key oils, cork grease, slide lubricants, and cleaning supplies such as swabs, mouthpiece brushes, and snakes. Include the types of sticks and mallets that will be needed by percussionists. This would also be a good time to include the list of method book(s) you will be using and any supplementary materials (such as a folding stand) the child will need.

"Many...manufacturers and publishers distribute their products through local retail dealers. These dealers can perform valuable and helpful services for you in recruiting beginners, repairing instruments, improving public relations, and perhaps obtaining the services of clinicians and consultants available from their suppliers. Learn to know these dealers."

—MUSIC INDUSTRY CONFERENCE
GUIDE FOR MUSIC EDUCATORS

Communicating with Students Continuing in the Program

If you are a new teacher in an existing program, in addition to preparing for the first beginner classes, you will need to find the students from the previous year. Do this as early as you can—preferably before school starts. If lists of students are not available, ask the principal, secretary, classroom teacher, or other music teachers for help. Look in the music room for grade or plan books to find enrollment lists from last year. Concert programs or talks with music dealers may be another source to help you find former students. Another idea is to have an announcement made over the intercom or to write a memo to the classroom teachers. At the secondary level, you may find that students are already enrolled for a new year.

The next step is to introduce yourself by letter or phone call and invite the students to continue in the program. If students have returned their instruments, you may have a real selling job to do. Listen to the students' reasons for dropping out, and enthusiastically encourage them to try it again. Tell them of the plans you have for the year—such as joint concerts with other schools or other special activities—but most important, stress that they are going to feel really special as advanced players in the school.

Once you start teaching the students, remember that they will naturally be loyal to their previous teacher. Don't regard their comments as negative to you personally. Respect the students' attitude, and do not criticize the former teacher's work. Focus on positive learning experiences and realize that it takes time for students to develop a loyalty to you. Be patient.

Communicating with Parents

As your enrollment shapes up and as the school year progresses, keep parents informed about your program. Send them written communications about:
• grading procedures
• practice expectations
• behavior policies
• concert dates and your expectations regarding attendance
• concert dress
• instrument care

If any students have problems with progress, behavior, attendance, and so forth, give the parents a call. They will be impressed by your professionalism and interest in their children. Also call parents of students who are doing exceptionally well. Let them know that their children are leaders (you may also want to suggest private lessons). Finally, give parents verbal progress reports at concerts. Describe briefly the skills (regarding styles, bowings, embouchure, and rhythms) that students have developed; also, identify the challenges of the selections to be performed.

Another forum for communication with parents is the "informance." This is more formal than a classroom visit but less formal than a concert. It should center around a performance of the literature being studied in your ensemble, and it should also include information about the process of learning that goes on in your rehearsals and the educational goals that you are striving to attain. The performance, which may or may not be polished, can demonstrate any of the techniques that you find most appropriate in your teaching.

Finally, you can help parents form an organization to assist with some of the nonteaching aspects of the program. Parents in such an organization can serve as a telephone committee, do public-relations work for the program, serve as chaperons for field trips, or take on fund-raising tasks if necessary. When working with this organization, you must take careful notes of the decisions of the group (or see that someone else takes notes.) If the group is involved in fund-raising, you will need to keep your principal informed of what is going on and keep careful, itemized records of all income and expenditures.

• • • • • • • • • • • • • • • • • •
Communicating with the Community

Publicity about performances, festivals, and other activities brings visibility to the instrumental music program. Human-interest stories about the students' daily routine, as well as insights about individual "cool" kids and their activities, can be included in news releases to local radio and TV stations, newspapers, the PTA, and school bulletins. An article about the recruitment for new students, accompanied by a photograph of the recruiting session, can be effective.

"*The primary criterion in establishing a school policy with respect to public performance must always be the educational value of the experience. It is important that the demands of public performances and competitive activities not be allowed to become dominant or excessive, and that public performances remain secondary to education in the curriculum. There should be no contradiction between the two because the former clearly supports the latter.*"

—Guidelines for Performances of
School Music Groups

Guidelines for Press Releases (Print Media)

- *Type the release, double spaced, with one-inch margins, on 8 1/2 X 11 paper, using a standard typeface and black type.*

- *List your ensemble and your name, address, title, and daytime telephone number (including area code) in the upper right corner of the first page. You should be prepared to supply further information on demand.*

- *Put "FOR IMMEDIATE RELEASE" in the upper left corner. Time the release so that it arrives at a daily newspaper at least one week before the date on which you want it used; for weeklies or magazines, you will have to allow considerably more lead time.*

- *Start the release with a short headline, supplying the "hook" for the story.*

Performances out in the community are also great public-relations tools. You may want to arrange them by developing a relationship with charitable or service organizations that may become supporters of your band or orchestra program. Once you begin to stage such performances, however, requests may flood in, so be selective! Remember that these kinds of performances are extensions of the program, not the purpose.

Encourage attendance at community orchestra and band concerts or consider contacting the management of your local symphony, youth orchestra, or community band to discuss possible "side-by-side" concerts.

Finally, remember that the strength of your instrumental program depends on the strength of the music program in general. If your area doesn't already have a coalition for music advocacy, talk to teachers, parents, music merchants, and others interested parties about forming one. Coalitions are not only for programs that are faced with budget cuts or cutbacks in scheduling; they are designed to maintain the strength of established programs as well.

Communicating with Your Professional Colleagues

As you complete each year, treat yourself by planning to attend a summer workshop—continuing to improve your skills as a teacher—and to make friends with other instrumental music teachers. Look in the professional journals of the Music Educators National Conference (or in the journals listed at the back of this book) for notices about summer workshops. Then don't worry about your students continuing in the program for another year. They will continue to play as long as they feel that they are learning, and as long as they are playing music that is fun and challenging and that makes them feel good about themselves. So, relax and have a good summer.

- *Begin the body of the release with a dateline (city of origin and date).*

- *The first paragraph of the release should include five things only: who, what, when, where, and why.*

- *Limit the release to one page if possible.*

- *Attach a personal note to the release to call attention to it and to set it apart from the dozens of other releases that editors and reporters receive daily.*

—ADAPTED FROM BUILDING SUPPORT FOR SCHOOL MUSIC

Success in the Business of Teaching

Understanding the Professional Environment

It is your responsibility to implement your program in a businesslike manner. To do this, you need to acquaint yourself with the professional environment of your school and community. You will need to be responsible for understanding school policies and procedures for student evaluation, attendance, record keeping, meetings, and teacher evaluation. You will also need to know what expectations your administrative supervisors and the community have for the program and understand the level of resources they are willing to provide for you.

You must also understand the religious, ethnic, and socioeconomic climate of all of your students. This understanding will help you avoid conflicts with important holidays or observances and will help you determine the amount of personal involvement and financial commitment that parents will be able to provide. Even more important, knowledge about the community in which you teach will help you to identify influential persons who may be called upon for help from time to time.

● ● ● ● ● ● ● ● ● ● ● ●

Planning Your Instructional Program

A major part of any business is planning. In the teaching field, your planning is long-range (involving the large dimensions of a well-rounded music program—band, orchestra, and choral activities), and short-range (involving daily rehearsals of each group). It is necessary that you prepare written lesson plans for each class, listing the goals and objectives for each class—identifying what is to be taught and how it is to be accomplished.

Curriculum. You should have a copy of the curriculum on file in your office as well as in the principal's office. If you don't have a written curriculum, develop one. (Refer to MENC's *Teaching Stringed Instruments: A Course of Study* or *Teaching Wind and Percussion Instruments: A Course of Study*.) Part of this record should be a written plan for a consistent grading procedure.

Student assessment and evaluation. This is one of the most difficult tasks facing any teacher. Grades should always recognize the progress of each student as well as the differences between students. In addition to keeping a written record of the grading procedure on file, you should let

21

students know at the beginning of the term what is expected of them and how they will be evaluated. This will cause the least amount of misunderstanding later when grading time comes around. Some directors give students a policy handbook at the beginning of the school year.

Grades in instrumental music need to reflect skill-based music curriculum requirements and be similar to the type of grading used in the other classes in the school. Parents should be notified immediately, by means of a phone call or a written note, when a child is having a problem. Reports to parents should always include suggestions for furthering progress.

Be sure to reward and recognize each step of a student's progress. This will prevent discouragement among the students. Many teachers use a special music grade card that lists techniques the students should be able to accomplish. It is also important for there to be a grade for band or orchestra on the regular academic report card.

Facilities, equipment, and supplies. Look at possible teaching spaces to ascertain what your needs will be. You will need:
• Adequate space for the largest class, preferably with a flat floor (no risers). If necessary, and with appropriate scheduling, the band and orchestra program could share the same space.
• A quiet rehearsal room, acoustically separate from other classrooms and away from noise.

• Sufficient chairs and music stands.
• A piano or electronic keyboard.
• A secure, adequate storage place. This should be neither excessively hot nor cold, and should have appropriate shelves, racks, or closets for all instruments.
• A teacher's desk.
• A chalkboard.
• Funds to purchase music.
• Access to a stereo system, including a cassette or CD player.

Itinerant teachers often have less than adequate teaching space. If you are faced with this problem, articulate your needs to the principal in terms of the impact on instruction. Let him or her know that you trust that every effort will be made to find the best possible place to teach. If your principal asks for exact specifications, show him or her the figures listed in the MENC publication, *Opportunity-to-Learn Standards for Music Instruction.*

Planning is the key. You must anticipate your future needs during budget preparation time. (Ask your principal when this time is.) Show appreciation for what has been provided, but continue to request what is important. Be patient. An ideal teaching environment may take years to develop. Consult the "Music Industry Conference Guide for Music Educators," published every other year in January as an insert in the *Music Educators Journal,* for assistance in this area.

Keeping Track

Records. As a teacher, you will be expected to keep accurate attendance and grade records. As the manager of an educational ensemble, you must also keep a personal calendar, an up-to-date concert and rehearsal calendar, and a schedule for use of the facilities under your direction. You must, of course, maintain inventory records for rental instruments, music from the library, uniforms, and other equipment. You may want to get copies of forms used in a school system with a high-quality band and orchestra program. You need to keep accurate records for all financial transactions. Some school systems require financial records to be kept in the principal's office.

Equipment. You will also need to monitor your stock of equipment closely. You should keep a master property list, with a description of each inventory item, its location (on site or on loan to a student), and its disposition (if sold or discarded). In addition, instruments, uniforms, or other items routinely lent to students should each be tracked with an issue record that lists the item, the student to whom it is loaned, its condition when loaned out, and its condition when returned.

Copyright. As a music educator, you have a special obligation to comply with all aspects of the law regarding the intellectual property of composers and arrangers. For the most part, this will entail obtaining licenses from copyright holders for four kinds of rights: rights to arrange works, rights to perform works, rights to record works, and rights to photocopy works.

Making an arrangement of a musical work requires prior permission from the owner of

"Under the U.S. Copyright Law, copyright owners have the exclusive right to print, publish, copy, and sell their protected works. The copyright owners of the books and music you purchase are indicated on those publications....Certain uses of copyrighted music may require prior clearance. To assist you in comprehending the situation concerning copyright and to facilitate clearance where necessary, the Music Publishers' Association has available, at no cost, the pamphlet "The United States Copyright Law: A Guide for Music Educators." This may be secured from the Music Publishers' Association of the United States, 205 East Forty-Second Street, New York, NY 10017."

—MUSIC INDUSTRY CONFERENCE
GUIDE FOR MUSIC EDUCATORS

the work. In contrast, the right to perform works in the course of normal instructional activities needs no permission. If you want to mount a performance that goes beyond the normal course of instruction, however, you must get permission to do so. Your right to record a concert is limited to making one archival recording; you need a "mechanical license" to produce or distribute any further audiotapes and a "synchronization license" to distribute additional videotapes. Every time you obtain one of these licenses, you must keep clear records of your actions.

Finally, the right to photocopy books or music is severely restricted by law. The best policy is never to allow students to play from photocopies—especially in performance. Exceptions in the law that allow photocopying for classroom use have to do with temporary, emergency copying of parts and with copying short segments of music for study (they must be too short to be performed). Violations will certainly lead to professional embarrassment and can lead to heavy fines, as well.

Remember, copyright is a complex and confusing issue. As a music educator, you will want to gain a basic knowledge of the legal issues involved, proceed with care in administering your program, and seek legal counsel when necessary.

Uniforms. Band and orchestra teachers may also need to monitor the assignment of uniforms. Working, if possible, two to three weeks before uniforms are issued, you should take chest, waist, trouser inseam, and hat measurements for each student. These measurements can be summarized for each component of the uniform (such as jacket, pants, skirts, or hat) on a uniform assignment chart.

Then, starting from the smallest size and moving upward, you can assign uniforms from inventory to students, making whatever adjustments or compromises are necessary to see that each student receives a reasonable fit. The *Music Booster Manual* has more suggestions and information on these topics.

End-of-year tasks. Here are tasks you will need to accomplish at the close of the school year:
• Inventory school-owned instruments and other equipment.
• Arrange for any needed repair of instruments.
• Prepare instruments for safe storage for the summer.
• Collect and file school-owned music.
• Check uniforms and arrange for cleaning and storage.
• Prepare a budget and plan purchasing for the new year.
• Notify music dealers of your needs (for method books, instruments, accessories, and so forth) for the next year.
• Plan a calendar for new year.
• Leave student records (such as class lists, grades, and curriculum materials) in appropriate offices.
• Pass on information (including class lists, grouping, and records of student progress) to the teacher who will have your students next year.

In the string orchestra, check and clean each instrument thoroughly. Note the condition of the pegs, the strings, the fingerboard, the bridge, the soundpost, the tuners, the tail loop, and the end button or end pin. Also check for any openings in seams or cracks in the instrument. *The Complete String Guide* has a useful checklist for this task.

In the band, woodwind instruments should be carefully checked to make sure all keys, pads, springs, and corks are in good working condition. Look for cracks in wooden piccolos, clarinets, oboes, and bassoons, and for any dents that may impair the playing of flutes and saxophones. Check all woodwind instruments to make sure that pads are seated correctly to avoid air leaks. Brass instruments should be checked to make sure all valves and slides move freely. Strings on valve rotors and spit valve assemblies should also be checked. Dents that impair the playing of brass instruments should be removed. Brass instruments need to be cleaned by flushing warm water through the tubing with a cleaning snake. Certain instruments may need to be acid-dipped for proper cleaning. If you have questions, contact a local instrument specialist for advice.

It is always a good idea to check the condition of all drum heads and rims, as well as mechanical assemblies such as snare throw-offs. You may also want to lubricate the drum lugs with grease to prevent rusting and to allow drum heads to be tuned.

● ● ● ● ● ● ● ● ● ● ● ● ● ●
Working as a Professional

The perception of you as a music teacher in your school can greatly influence your effectiveness. To have a professional image, you must:
- Present yourself professionally in dress, language, and manner at all times.
- Arrive on time for classes, meetings, and other assignments.
- Organize your materials and time effectively.
- Remember that you are a teacher, not a "buddy" to the students.
- Write communications that are clear and correct.
- Work with your local music dealers.
- Make prior arrangements for substitutes as needed.
- Engage in lifelong learning.
- Stay current on music and education trends.
- Join and participate in professional organizations.
- Attend professional conferences and workshops to continue learning.
- Continue to be an active performing musician.

In addition to maintaining a professional image, you need to consider the professional ethics that apply to your work as an instrumental director. Some important guidelines:
- Recommend more than one private teacher or music dealer.
- Never accept commissions from dealers, manufacturers, or any other source.

*"**A**ll fund-raising efforts should adhere to responsible standards of safety and well being for the students. It is important that ethical and legal implications of the project be thoroughly understood in order to prevent jeopardizing the music teacher or program and to avoid situations which might result in litigation due to an accident or other misfortune."*

—MENC Position Statement on Fund-raising

• Know your district's policy for private instruction of students enrolled in your program and the use of school facilities for such instruction.

• Consult with administration in all financial matters, including record keeping and audits, fund-raising activities, and contributions for student performances in the community.

• Do not use students in a venue that could displace professional musicians. Consult the *Music Code of Ethics* (available from MENC). Basically, the code puts forth the idea that educational institutions should not interfere with the livelihood of professionals. Teachers should devote their educational efforts to the task of teaching students and to the activities that are a logical extension of that task.

• Learn and observe copyright laws (see page 23).

• Be sensitive about information that should be kept confidential and that which needs to be communicated to parents or administration. You will need to become familiar with state law and school policies regarding student confidentiality, sexual harassment, substance abuse, and child abuse.

SUCCESSFUL CONCEPTS FOR TEACHING

● ● ● ● ● ● ● ● ● ● ● ● ●

Axioms for Success

Success breeds success. Basically, students will continue in a group that sounds good and where they are continually learning and improving their playing skills.

Successful and creative teachers use a variety of techniques to reach students. The teaching style you adopt will depend on your background, your situation, and most of all your students. There are, however, a number of ideas about which educators universally agree:

Teach only one new thing at a time. Isolate skills when the music calls for more than one thing at a time.

Talk as little as possible. Use nonverbal teaching (demonstration or manual assistance). As a guideline, spend at least 75 percent of the lesson time playing.

Introduce new techniques by rote—away from the music. Demonstrate a skill and ask the students to imitate it. Music reading follows the mastery of skills learned by rote. Even after note reading has been introduced, it is a good idea to have the students count or sing lines in rhythm before playing.

Keep in mind that mastery of skills is important from the very beginning and never forget that the most basic skills will need constant review. Use repetition to help students master new techniques. With creative repetition (and when students know what they are trying to accomplish), necessary drill becomes interesting. Faulty practice leads to bad playing habits that are sometimes impossible to break.

Remind students and their parents that quality of practice is more important than quantity. Use the school lesson as a model for home practice. Home practice should be on material studied in class. (Telling students "Go on to the next page" is not appropriate.)

Establish a routine for rehearsing. Set a pace that keeps students challenged, but one that is not so fast that they will feel discouraged. When you hit a stumbling block, analyze the situation: Are you moving too fast? Did you skip a step? Are you asking students to do more than one thing at a time? Don't blame the students for the problem. To keep them excited and engaged, try alternating whole-group playing with brief segments of small-group and individual playing.

Choose music that is not too difficult, and allow plenty of time to prepare performance music. Always start rehearsals with well-established skills or concepts, moving from the known or old material to the unknown or new

> **"As** *music teachers, we have always been involved with the teaching of thinking skills. We have just called it by a different name, musicianship. While our classroom colleagues deal primarily with the world of verbal discourse, we develop a similar set of intellectual skills through the medium of music.* **"**
>
> —Dimensions of Musical Thinking

material. As you do this, foster critical thinking and listening skills. Ask questions about what and why, rather than simply giving the information.

Public performance determines the image and future of the program. Be sure to present polished performances. Work, however, to teach beyond the concert—all components of a quality music education should be included in an instrumental program. You should help your students excel in tone production and quality, technique, ear training, music reading and vocabulary, and in music theory and music history.

Don't shortchange the potential of your students and your program: in addition to the obviously important process of familiarizing students with great composers from the Western tradition, broaden their horizons by presenting an international theme for a concert. It is also important that you let the audience in on what, why, and how your students are learning. This will help them have a greater appreciation of what it is that you are doing in class and will build strong support for your program in the community.

Believe that the students have unlimited potential. Their achievement will be only as high as your expectations. Give individuals help and encouragement as the group plays. Reward improvement with positive reinforcement.

As you work to motivate the students, keep your own perspective, a positive attitude, and good humor. Enjoy and be enthusiastic about your work. Remember, the goal is to develop communication and sensitivity through the language of music.

In the string orchestra: With young players, it is most important for the teacher to model a beautiful sound and correct position at every lesson. (Position of the instrument is critical, and it must look right to sound right.) Do not introduce music reading until the left-hand and right-hand skills are set; however, don't delay music reading so long that students find it difficult. Playing pizzicato before bowing is also a good idea.

In the band: Young students must first learn the correct way to assemble their instruments. Without good assembly habits they can have problems with bent keys, dented brass instruments, or cracked woodwind mouthpieces. Next, teachers must demonstrate (and students must learn) correct hand position, embouchure, and posture. Teachers must repeatedly demonstrate correct breathing techniques prior to making the first sounds on the instruments. Whenever possible, it is good for teachers or advanced students to demonstrate good characteristic sounds for the beginning students to emulate.

● ● ● ● ● ● ● ● ● ● ● ● ● ● ● ●

Working with Faster-Moving or Advanced Students

Thinking of creative ways to challenge advanced students while giving enough time and repetition for slower-moving students is an important part of the art of teaching. It is your responsibility to provide every student with the opportunity to learn.

If you are fortunate to have some advanced students in your ensemble, you will need to use additional strategies to serve their educational needs. Some ideas include providing positive reinforcement and recognition for

"Although each component will not necessarily receive equal time during instruction, each must be present. Students are short-changed when one aspect is emphasized over another."

—TEACHING STRINGED INSTRUMENTS:
A COURSE OF STUDY

the students' accomplishments, giving them (and your program) an additional boost by letting them help you recruit new students, and using them as models of good sound and technique. (Of course, you must recognize the need for them to be accepted socially as part of the group.)

Your first responsibility is to assess the advanced students' ability levels and needs. To do this, talk to their parents and private teachers so that everyone connected with the students can work together to nurture their abilities. Remember in these discussions that your class offers the reading and ensemble skills that they need for full musical development. Encourage private study so that these students will have the additional challenge of supervised solo playing.

Other good ideas are to use advanced or fast-moving students as mentors. You can also give advanced students an independent project to work on while you work with others who need more help. Challenge them by having them play with advanced techniques (alternate fingerings for winds, in higher positions or with vibrato for strings) while the others do the material an easier way. Place fast-moving students in chamber music groups or small ensembles to give them extra opportunities to refine their skills.

● ● ● ● ● ● ● ● ● ● ● ● ● ● ● ●
Working with Students Who Need More Help

If your program is to provide the environment for all students to grow and develop, you will need supportive strategies for students who do not progress as quickly as others. Moving on to new ideas before the old ones are mastered invites failure. Failure discourages learning and produces drop-outs. Give every child the time to learn by:
• Reviewing skills learned previously
• Teaching only one new thing at a time
• Providing a student buddy or mentor
• Presenting instruction in different ways
• Consulting with the student's parents
• Encouraging private study

Designing Success: A Sequence for Teaching

● ● ● ● ● ● ● ● ● ● ● ●

Scheduling

A number of successful patterns exist for scheduling band and orchestra programs. To find one that meets the needs of your school system, you will need to make three decisions.

First, in what grade should the program begin? MENC suggests that string instrument instruction begin no later than grade five and wind instrument instruction no later than grade six—but there are some successful programs that begin instruction earlier, and some that start at the middle school level.

Second, how often should classes meet? Band or orchestra classes should meet at least two times a week. Ideally, they should meet at least three times a week for a minimum of thirty-five minutes per session. Frequency of instruction is particularly critical in the first year for string students.

Third, when should instruction take place? Instruction should take place during the regular school day, but there are many possible schedules that can be used. At the elementary level,

you can use a rotating schedule that allows students to be taken from other subjects only once in several weeks. A schedule that allows band and orchestra to meet at the same time minimizes interruptions for the classroom teacher.

At the middle school or high school levels, most successful programs meet as regularly scheduled classes at least two or three times a week. Rehearsal time should total at least 120 minutes a week. Instruction at this level should include technical development on an individual instrument (a rotating lesson schedule may be used) and large ensemble experience in a band or orchestra that performs appropriate literature.

If seventh-grade instrumental students are expected to perform in a band or orchestra at an intermediate level, instruction should begin in grade four or five for strings and grade five or six for band. The grouping of grade levels in your school system as a whole will be a major concern as you plan what ensembles you will offer at each level.

In the string orchestra, consider these facts: stringed instruments are available in small sizes, making it possible for young children to begin playing. Also, playing a stringed instrument necessitates adequate instructional time for establishing good habits in the beginning stages.

In the band, remember that there are as many as fifteen wind instruments being taught plus the various percussion instruments. In many cases it may be necessary to get students to switch to another instrument in order to achieve an acceptable instrumentation so that good band literature can be introduced. Additional instruction and assistance must be provided for those students who elect to change instruments.

● ● ● ● ● ● ● ● ● ● ● ● ● ●
Final Preparations

Planning a logical teaching sequence that meets the needs of all your students is one of the central challenges of being a band or orchestra director. First, have the rehearsal room ready for instruction before the students arrive for the first class, with the chairs, music stands, music, tuner, and so on, all ready for use. Materials you may wish to have ready include:
• Your demonstration instrument
• Your lesson plan
• A teacher's manual and music lesson plans
• Roll book
• Practice records
• Handouts to students or parents
• Pencils
• Tuning device
• CD or cassette player
• Music books or music literature
• Music folders (if needed)

In the string orchestra, you may also want to be ready with sponges and rubber bands or shoulder pads, extra strings and rosin, cello and bass end pin stops, pliers, and a chin-rest tightening device, as well as a spare violin, viola, and cello. See *Teaching*
Stringed Instruments: A Course of Study for more information.

In the band, you may want to have on hand some valve oil, slide grease, a mouthpiece puller, some extra clarinet and saxophone reeds, and a disinfectant for mouthpieces. Some emergency spring problems can be temporarily remedied with a rubber band; however, it is important that the spring be fixed correctly as soon as possible so the rubber band does not tarnish the brass. It can also be helpful to have an assortment of pads and corks available for emergencies. Be sure to disinfect students' mouthpieces before and after playing them, and remind students that using another's mouthpiece without first disinfecting it is similar to using someone else's toothbrush. See *Teaching Wind and Percussion Instruments: A Course of Study* for more information.

● ● ● ● ● ● ● ● ● ● ● ● ● ●
Tuning

Tuning is the beginning of the music class. Tune as quickly as possible and maximize time for developing skills and knowledge. Establish effective class discipline. Expect students to be quiet during tuning. Establish a routine for tuning, and use correct, standard pitch every day. (Use a piano, tuning fork, pitch pipe, or electronic tuner.)

In the string orchestra:
• Be sure all beginner violins, violas, and cellos have steel strings, fine tuners, and well-fitted ebony pegs.

- Tune the instruments ahead of time if possible.
- Try to use no more than five minutes to tune. (Of course this varies with the size of the class; however, once the instruments have been tuned for several weeks, they will stay in tune longer and less time will be needed for tuning.)
- Teach students to tune their own instruments as soon as they can hear the correct pitches and have the strength to handle the pegs without breaking the strings.

In the band: The first rule of tuning is, "You cannot tune and talk!" Tuning requires concentration and listening; these require silence. It is essential that students play with correct embouchure, hand position, posture, and breath support. Good intonation is not likely if the instruments are not being played correctly.

- Be certain your young brass players are playing the correct partial (the correct harmonic).
- Since young wind players are using new muscles that take time to develop, it may be very difficult for them to alter their pitch at first. The key here is to reinforce good playing habits and help them learn to listen and try to match pitches.
- Students playing band instruments need to be taught the basics of tuning their instruments as soon as possible. They must learn to listen to each and every note, and try to adjust it by using compensating slides, alternate fingerings, or an adjustment of the embouchure.
- Since band classes are frequently taught in rooms that are too small, and the sounds are quite loud, some students may try to play softly using improper breath support or breathing habits. This must be carefully

"*Announce, establish, and enforce efficient classroom routines that all ensemble members must follow. Plan procedures for distributing music....In a rehearsal, listen and analyze what is happening constantly so that when there is a pause, you can quickly direct the students' attention to a particular problem. If you are slow to think and react, time is wasted and problems can arise.*"

—TIPS: DISCIPLINE IN THE MUSIC CLASSROOM

monitored to prevent the development of bad habits. One suggestion for addressing this problem is to say: "Inhale, take in a lot of air and hold it; then play softly." A good soft sound on a wind instrument requires a full supply of air.

•••••••••••••••••
The First Class

The first class is special, as it sets the example for the year. This class should be rigorous and enjoyable for the students. Because some students may not have instruments yet, you should be prepared to teach all the students something. For the first class you should be prepared to:

- Follow an efficient, accurate tuning procedure.
- Teach the students about such things as packing, unpacking, and carrying their instruments; care of their instruments; parts of their instruments; and holding their instruments.
- Provide a musical experience for every student. Some ideas include learning how to keep a steady beat (clapping and counting); doing some singing; and listening to you model a beautiful sound.
- Remind students of the next lesson time and what they will need to bring.
- Speak with students who did not have instruments at the end of class to find out why. Get phone numbers of these students and call their parents.

In the string orchestra, you can use this lesson to help the students learn the open strings or play pizzicato.

In the band, teach students proper assembly of their instruments, correct hand position, and good posture. Work on breathing, and if at all possible, set as many embouchures as possible and get the students to play their first sounds.

•••••••••••••••••
The First Few Sessions for Continuing Students

Students need to play music they know and enjoy as soon as possible. Ideas for this are:

- Warm up with echo patterns (you play; the students imitate) and rote scales.
- Play melodic unison songs that are within the students' technical abilities.
- Structure review of skills previously learned.

It may take several class periods before you can accurately assess the technical level of the students who have played before. Because of this, don't ask students and parents to purchase a new book for the year until you have had time to decide on the materials that will best serve the class. It is important to choose materials that include technical material, melodic material, and ensemble music in a mixture of review material and some new techniques.

Guidelines for Student Achievement

- Play music with slurs and ties.
- Play at different dynamic levels.
- Play some familiar unison melodies and possibly one or two simple, harmonized orchestrations.
- Cover most of Book One of a string or band method (this depends on the grade level and number of class meetings per week).

Students should also take part in performances including:

- A demonstration program for parents (as early in the year as possible so parents are aware of what students are learning).
- A spring concert, featuring the band, orchestra, and chorus, for the school and parents.
- A late spring concert combining like groups from several schools.
- A concert for potential beginners for the next year, including an informal presentation about how they can begin.

Classes for the First Year

In the band and string ensembles, continuously model good sound, proper hand position, posture, and breathing techniques.

By the end of the first year, students should be able to:

- Play with good holding position and correct left- and right-hand positions (strings).
- Play with good hand position, posture, embouchure, and breath support (winds).
- Play with a steady beat.
- Play with accurate intonation.
- Read notes and understand first-position notes in the key of D major and perhaps G major and C major (strings).
- Read notes and understand key signatures and accidentals covered in the beginning band and orchestra method materials.
- Play music with time signatures of 4/4, 3/4, and 2/4.
- Play music that utilizes quarter notes, half notes, dotted half notes, whole notes, along with the corresponding rests.

Classes for the Second Year

In the second year of instruction the class should focus on:

- Reviewing and refining all previously learned technical skills
- Introducing new skills—this would include approximately half or two-thirds of the total instruction time—including new keys, rhythms, and time signatures.
- Developing facility (playing faster and with more control).
- Progressing in musical understanding and expressive playing.

- Playing ensemble music that reinforces the technical skills the students are learning.
- Playing exercises or warm-ups related
to technical problems (rhythm patterns, key signatures, and so forth)
found in band or orchestra music.

More than ever, your class should be
the model for what the students are
expected to work on in home practice.
Good sound and intonation, effortless
playing, and joyful music making
should always be the primary goals.

In the string orchestra, there will
need to be much work on new bowing
techniques and styles, as well as new
finger patterns.

In the band, there will need to be
additional work on different kinds of
articulations and the development of
range and finger technique on each
instrument.

● ● ● ● ● ● ● ● ● ● ● ● ● ● ●
Classes for Third- and Fourth-Year Students

At this level, instruction should
focus on:
- A greater emphasis on the real band
and orchestra literature. (Choose
music of good quality, from a variety
of styles and musical periods.)
- A balance between development of
unison technical skills and the playing of music that reinforces the skills
being learned in the technique books.
- Continuation of unison playing to
gain better control of a beautiful
tone.

- Enrichment experiences (small-
ensemble playing; solo opportunities;
festival participation on the district,
county, and state levels; and community youth orchestras and bands).

In the string orchestra, try offering your students the opportunity to
participate in combined performances
with a youth orchestra, with string
orchestras from other schools (especially at other levels), with a full
orchestra, or with the school chorus.

In the band, provide enrichment
opportunities by utilizing high school
band students or community bands.
Invite the younger students to play in a
concert with the high school band, or
have the high school band play one of
the younger students' pieces with
them. Seat the younger musicians next
to the older ones.

Other ideas might involve the
younger students in a high school foot-
ball or basketball half-time show or
variety show. Local service clubs frequently provide a wonderful audience
for young musicians, as do nursing
homes. Such performance opportunities also are public-relations tools that
encourage continued community support for the music program.

Classes for Advanced Students (Fifth Year and Beyond)

At this level, it is appropriate to place a greater emphasis on the rehearsal and performance of litera-ture, as opposed to unison technical materials. Most groups use materials of this type mostly for warm-ups or as needed to assist with performance music. Continued enrichment experi-ences are essential to a substantive, successful band and orchestra experi-ence for the students. Rehearsals and performances with a guest conductor, guest clinician, or guest artist are great motivators for more advanced groups. For further detail on technical develop-ment at all levels, refer to MENC's *Teaching Stringed Instruments: A Course of Study* and *Teaching Wind and Percussion Instruments: A Course of Study.*

Classes at All Levels

Encourage private study to develop the students' full potential and build leaders for the band and orchestra. Identify competent private teachers and provide a list of these teachers to students and parents. Maintain commu-nication with private teachers.

You will need to work continually to create a healthy attitude among the stu-dents regarding seating, competition, and cooperation. Be sure to realize that the social aspect of music making is a powerful motivator, and use this aspect to make your rehearsals more successful. Ways to foster this are exchange concerts; shared perfor-mances with more advanced (or less advanced) ensembles; asking older stu-dents to assist younger students; taking part in sports activities and games; pizza parties, picnics, and skating par-ties; and adopting a simple casual uni-form such as special T-shirts, jackets, or sweatshirts.

EPILOGUE

Successful band and orchestra programs are marked by quality, planned with professionalism, taught by professionals who follow an effective sequence of instruction, and developed by those professionals with the cooperation and support of the entire school and community. When all of these elements come together, the success of the program is mirrored in the success of the students. The students find success in the discipline of practice and performance and in the development of academic and cognitive skills that they carry through their school years and into the years beyond.

These same students find in band and orchestra a foundation for a lifetime of enjoyment. It is this sense of joy in music making that is the most important contribution of the school music program to the nation. It is what enables students to live up to the standards set by the school and by the world at large. It is what helps students understand our culture and attain their places in our society.

"*The more students live up to these high expectations, the more empowered our citizenry will become.*"

—NATIONAL STANDARDS FOR
ARTS EDUCATION

SELECTED RESOURCES

● ● ● ● ● ● ● ● ● ● ● ●
Books and Articles

Boardman, Eunice, ed. *Dimensions of Musical Thinking.* Reston, VA: Music Educators National Conference, 1989.

Chusmir, Marsha. "Teaching Strings: A Special Opportunity for Wind and Percussion Majors." *American String Teacher* 24, no. 3 (1974): 6.

The Complete String Guide. Reston, VA: Music Educators National Conference, 1988.

Culver, Robert. "Goals of a String Program." *American String Teacher* 31, no. 3 (1981): 21–24.

Culver, Robert. "Survivors: Quality School Orchestra Programs." *American String Teacher* 34, no. 2 (1984): 42–43.

Dillon, Jacquelyn A. "Building and Maintaining Your String Program: Getting the Students You Need." *Music Performance Resource* (Spring 1988).

Dillon, Jacquelyn A. "How to Educate Parents for a Better String Program." In *Voices of Industry.* Reston, VA: Music Educators National Conference, 1990.

Dillon, Jacquelyn A. "Schools Should Orchestrate Orchestras." In *Conn Chord.* Elkhart, IN: C. G. Conn, 1978.

Dillon, Jacquelyn A. "Twenty Tips for Successful String Class Recruiting." *Orchestra News* 17, no. 1 (Spring 1979).

Dillon, Jacquelyn A. "What Is Your Recruiting Quotient?" *American String Teacher* 30, no. 2 (1980): 24.

Dillon, Jacquelyn A., and Casimer Kriechbaum. *How to Design and Teach a Successful School String and Orchestra Program.* San Diego: Kjos West, 1978.

Dillon-Krass, Jacquelyn, and Dorothy A. Straub, comps. *TIPS: Establishing a String and Orchestra Program.* Reston, VA: Music Educators National Conference, 1991.

Edwards, Arthur C. *Beginning String Class Method.* Dubuque, IA: William C. Brown, 1985.

Englehardt, D. "Successful Beginning String Programs." *The Instrumentalist* 31 (September 1979): 36–37.

Evans, Judith. "The Importance of a Good Instrument to the Success of the Beginner." *Orchestra News* 17, no. 1 (Spring 1979).

Green, Barry, and W. Timothy Gallwey. *The Inner Game of Music.* New York: Doubleday, 1986.

Green, Elizabeth. *Guide to Orchestral Bowings.* American String Teachers Association, 1987.

Green, Elizabeth. *The Modern Conductor.* 4th ed. Englewood Cliffs, NJ: Prentice-Hall, 1987.

Green, Elizabeth A. H. *Teaching String Instruments in Classes.* American String Teachers Association, 1987.

Guidelines for Performances of School Music Groups. Reston, VA: Music Educators National Conference, 1986.

Herriagal, Eugene. *Zen in the Art of Teaching.* New York: Random House, 1971.

Hunsberger, Donald, and Roy Ernst. *The Art of Conducting.* New York: Alfred A. Knopf, 1983.

Iams, C. Gary. "Recruiting Strings." In *The Best of Soundpost.* Pittsburgh: National School Orchestra Association, 1976.

Kjelland, James. "String-o-Phobia: Some Causes and Cures." *American String Teacher* 37, no. 2 (1987): 70–74.

Klotman, Robert. *Teaching Strings.* New York: G. Schirmer, 1988.

Kriechbaum, Casimer, and Kay Kirtley. "How to Recruit String Students for a String Program." *Orchestra News* 16, no. 2 (Fall 1978).

Kreines, Joseph. *Music for Concert Band: A Selective Annotated Guide to Band Literature.* Tampa, FL: Florida Music Service, 1989.

Lamb, Norman. *Guide to Teaching Strings.* 4th ed. Dubuque, IA: William C. Brown, 1984.

Matesky, Ralph. *Playing and Teaching Stringed Instruments.* 2 vols. Englewood Cliffs, NJ: Prentice Hall, 1963.

McElheran, Brock. *Conducting Technique for Beginners and Professionals.* New York: Oxford University Press, 1966.

"MENC's Position Statement on Fund-raising." *MENC Soundpost* (Fall 1991): 15.

Meyer, R. F. *The Band Director's Guide to Instrument Repair.* Van Nuys, CA: Alfred, 1973.

Mullins, Shirley. *Teaching Music: The Human Experience.* Willow Park, TX: Media Services, 1985.

Music Booster Manual. Reston, VA: Music Educators National Conference, 1989.

"Music Industry Conference Guide for Music Educators." A supplement to *Music Educators Journal* (January 1993).

National Coalition for Music Education. *Building Support for School Music.* Reston, VA: Music Educators National Conference, 1991.

National Standards for Arts Education. Reston, VA: Music Educators National Conference, 1994.

Oddo, Vincent. *Playing and Teaching the Strings.* Belmont, CA: Wadsworth, 1979.

Opportunity-to-Learn Standards for Music Instruction. Reston, VA: Music Educators National Conference, 1994.

Rabin, Marvin, and Priscilla Smith. *Guide to Orchestral Bowing through Musical Styles.* Madison, WI: University of Wisconsin Press, 1984.

Reimer, Bennett. *A Philosophy of Music Education.* Englewood Cliffs, NJ: Prentice Hall, 1970.

Rossman, R. Lewis, comp. *TIPS: Discipline in the Music Classroom.* Reston, VA: Music Educators National Conference, 1989.

The School Music Program: A New Vision. Reston, VA: Music Educators National Conference, 1994.

Stycos, R. *School Orchestra Director's Guide.* Portland, ME: Western Walch, 1982.

Suzuki, Shinichi. *Nurtured by Love: The Classic Approach to Talent Education.* Athens, OH: Accura Music, 1987.

Teaching Stringed Instruments: A Course of Study. Reston, VA: Music Educators National Conference, 1991.

Teaching Wind and Percussion Instruments: A Course of Study. Reston, VA: Music Educators National Conference, 1991.

Voices of Industry. Reston, VA: Music Educators National Conference, 1990.

Wallace, David, and Eugene Corporan. *Wind Ensemble/Band Repertoire.* Greeley, CO: University of Northern Colorado School of Music, 1984.

Witt, Anne C. *Recruiting for the School Orchestra.* Elkhart, IN: The Selmer Company, 1984.

Young, Phyllis. *Playing the String Game: Strategies for Teaching Cello and Strings.* Austin, TX: University of Texas Press, 1978.

● ● ● ● ● ● ● ● ● ● ● ● ● ● ●
Periodicals

American Music Teacher
Music Teachers National Association
441 Vine St., Ste 505
Cincinnati, OH 45202-2811

American String Teacher
American String Teachers Association
4153 Chain Bridge Rd.
Fairfax, VA 22030

The Instrumentalist
200 Northfield Road
Northfield, IL 60093

Music Educators Journal
The National Association for Music Education
1806 Robert Fulton Dr.
Reston, VA 20191

Teaching Music
The National Association for Music Education
1806 Robert Fulton Dr.
Reston, VA 20191

● ● ● ● ● ● ● ● ● ● ● ● ● ●
Professional Associations

The American Bandmasters Association
2221 Morgan Drive
Norman, OK 73069-6528

American School Band Directors Association
227 North 1st Street
P.O. Box 696
Guttenberg, IA 52052

American String Teachers
Association
4153 Chain Bridge Rd.
Fairfax, VA 22030

American Symphony Orchestra
League
1156 Fifteenth Street NW, Suite 800
Washington, DC 20005-1704

College Band Directors National
Association
University of Texas
Box 8028
Austin, TX 78712-1026

International Association of Jazz
Educators
PO Box 724
Manhattan, KS 66502

Music Teachers National Association
441 Vine St., Ste 505
Cincinnati, OH 45202-2811

The National Association for Music
Education
1806 Robert Fulton Dr.
Reston, VA 20191

National Band Association
PO Box 121292
Nashville, TN 37212

Suzuki Association of the Americas
PO Box 17310
Boulder, CO 80308

Women Band Directors International
322 Overlook Drive
West Lafayette, IN 47906

LIST OF CONTRIBUTORS

*The material in this book originated in a series of
meetings of the MENC Ad Hoc Committee
on String and Orchestra Education.
Committee members include:*

Tanya Carey, Suzuki Association of the Americas

Jeff Cox, Suzuki Association of the Americas

Robert Culver, American String Teachers Association

Sandra Dackow, National School Orchestra Association

Jacquelyn Dillon-Krass, American String Teachers Association

Gerald Doan, American String Teachers Association

Jim Eaton, Music Industry Council

Catherine French, American Symphony Orchestra League

Robert Greenwood, National School Orchestra Association

Jerry Kupchynsky, National School Orchestra Association

Harriet Mogge, Music Educators National Conference

Harold Popp, School of Music, Wichita (Kansas) State University

Dorothy A. Straub, Music Educators National Conference

Anne Witt, American String Teachers Association

Arlene Witte, National School Orchestra Association

Ideas for band directors were supplied by:

Bob Foster, National Band Association

Charles T. Menghini, Olathe North (Kansas) High School